Presented To:

_____

By:

_____

Date:

_____

ACKNOWLEDGEMENTS

We gratefully recognize
the work of:
Illustrations Elements & Chickypooh
By: The JC Collection
Cora Artz, Editor
Copyright ©2016 by Jacqueline
Charmane
The JC Collection
www.chickypooh.com

ISBN: 978-0-9974496-2-4

Here we go again, thought
Chickypooh, as she walked out her
front door. The stench is so strong
it makes her gasp trying to head
toward the store.

Whoever you are with that awful
smell, please get out of my way. I
hope you know that smoking can
prevent you from living another day.

Chickypooh heard a chuckle then two coughs coming from a cloud of smoke. Believe you me, she said, it's a warning sign for your health when you choke.

Warning of what, asked Big C, with his deep raspy voice. I know the law and I know that smoking is my choice.

Don't point your finger, he said, as though you have only ever been nice. When you were younger, you probably got caught smoking at least once or twice.

I don't smoke! proclaimed Chickypooh. I never did and I never will. The odor that's left in your mouth smells like a rusted barbeque grill.

A smoker's lips are pale and gray, their teeth are no longer white. I always wonder if they know that it's not a pretty sight.

I don't need an X-Ray to find that their lungs have turned charcoal black. One day they may need a machine to help them breathe while they cough and hack.

If they dress up wearing perfume so sweet, to go somewhere grand. One puff on a cigarette or blunt and they'll smell like a rotting trash can.

Smoke has a way of attaching itself to everything it linkers near. Clothes, car, curtains and walls but that's not your worst fear.

Smoking changes your skin, teeth, and hair in ways that adds years to your looks. It also affects your heart, lungs, and bones while stealing from your pocketbook.

Smoking is a hard habit to quit but it's way too expensive to not. It used to be twenty-five cents for a pack, but now, well over five dollars it's shot.

You might as well be burning money which is insane to do so to say the least. For hungry children, that money could provide a meal equal to a Thanksgiving feast.

"I've been smoking for years, Big C interrupted, and have tried many times to stop!" Each time I made it two days but by the third my efforts would flop.

Because I haven't been able to quit, I just keep puffing away. I spend additional money on in halers, and breath and body sprays.

To disguise my shameful habit, chewing gum, candy and mints are also what I need to take. They all add to the cavities in the two teeth I have left. The rest of my teeth are fake.

WORLD NEWS

SMOKING ADVERTISEMENT BANDED 1970'S

How did you come to smoke asked Chickypooh listening with amaze. Surely, you were taught that smoking is not just a craze.

There used to be advertisement on TV and in magazines, showing people with cigarette packs. But they started banning them in the early 1970's because of the Public Health Act.

I've been around people who smoked, Big C replied, since the day I was born. I suffered from the dangers of second-hand smoke for which they were warned.

At first, I'd sneak a cigarette from a pack lying on the table. By the time I was sixteen, I'd ask a neighbor to purchase them since by law I was unable.

Smoking made me seem popular at first as the cool kids in school hung together. Then I realized that all we really were just birds of the same feather.

Smoking, drinking, and skipping school were what we did the most. Don't get me wrong. I don't say any of this to brag or boast.

I saw smoking as a way to be cool, to avoid becoming a square. But I had it all wrong. Smoking is a terrible habit that I wish I'd learned to beware.

I know longer have the right to smoke in most public places. If I do walk by someone while smoking, they make disgusted faces.

What would've been cool was for me to stay in school, so I could do the best I can. Taking care of my body and respecting others' health is by all means a better plan.

Every so often I see those classmates who I thought were squares and not cool. But they did their work, achieved good grades and graduated from high school.

Some are now in college, pursuing their goals and dreams. Unfortunately, smoking robbed me of mine, along with my self-esteem.

I'm relieved to finally talk to someone about how I've been feeling inside. Please help me to change my life for the better, help me restore my dignity and pride.

I'll gladly give you my advice, Chickypooh said, based on knowledge I've received. But the only way it will work for you is if you, too, believe.

It's not a simple task to accomplish but it's very simple to begin. You have to focus on the effects of smoking and allow them to Get Under Your Skin.

By Get Under Your Skin I mean they need to make you mad and annoy you very much. When you're disturbed by the effects of smoking then cigarettes and joints you surely won't touch.

Everything can influence you during this trial, either hindering or helping you to win. Listen closely to divine and spiritual lessons that are designed to guide you from within

There're going to be places where you can't go. These places will be obvious you'll see. Go where there's tranquil and pleasant vibes, such as the beach, where you can relax and feel free.

Avoid confrontations and stress that can lead to you craving nicotine once more. Instead, try exciting new things. It's easier when your life isn't a bore.

Laughter makes a weary soul to rejoice especially during solemn times. You'll be surprise how it really helps more than ever when you don't have even a dime.

Keeping your hands from becoming idle everyday will help you find your passion. Put the needs of others before your own which will bring about compassion.

If your friends continue smoking while you're attempting to quit. The best solution would be to get away from them. Get your things and split.

A support group is always helpful to identify the pits before you fall. You'll meet new people and make new friends you can count on and even call.

Each day you go without smoking, your senses will become more aware. You'll see, taste, touch, hear, and smell things that you never realized were there.

Pay close attention to your surroundings, seeing them as if they're new. It's the big, as well as little, changes that will help you make it through.

Your sense of taste before was distorted by nicotine destroying your palette. Once you quit, you'll begin to enjoy the simplest things, even a fresh garden salad.

It's important to remember that your journey can sometimes be a very lonely path. If you feel discouraged, just think of how many days you've been smoke free by doing the math.

SMOKE-FREE DAYS

SUNDAY	MONDAY	TUESDAY	WEDNESDAY	THURSDAY	FRIDAY	SATURDAY
				1	2	3
4	5	6	7	8	9	10
11	12	13	14	15	16	17
18	19	20	21	22	23	24
25	26	27	28	29	30	31

Last but not least, you will likely become very sensitive to smell. Without your nose dulled by smoke, odors in cars, homes, and clothes you will now be able to tell.

Let your renewed senses keep you on the right track. Just remember how bad it would feel if you slipped and went back.

Back is the operative word here. Don't let what's behind you hold you back any longer. No matter how many times you need to start over, each time you will become stronger.

If you talk to those who have quit, you will hear about some wonderful new beginnings. Let their stories inspire you that, even if it takes you several times, smoking doesn't have to be your ending.

So, please apply what I've shared with you to help you quit smoking. Let this be the very last time I hear you coughing and choking.

Step by step and day by day you'll get much stronger. Soon, one day, you'll realize that you crave cigarettes no longer.

Keep your head high. Don't ever give up, and remember to believe in your dreams. You can do it. I know, you can, no matter how hard it may seem.

You'll look back on the years that you let pass you by. Knowing now what you're able to achieve whatever you try.

I'll leave you a Chickypooh message to keep in mind with my hope and my prayer: Abstain from these pitfalls by saying NO. Life will challenge you; so, beware!

Make the choice to be and to stay smoke-free. Allow your life to be a positive example for others to see.

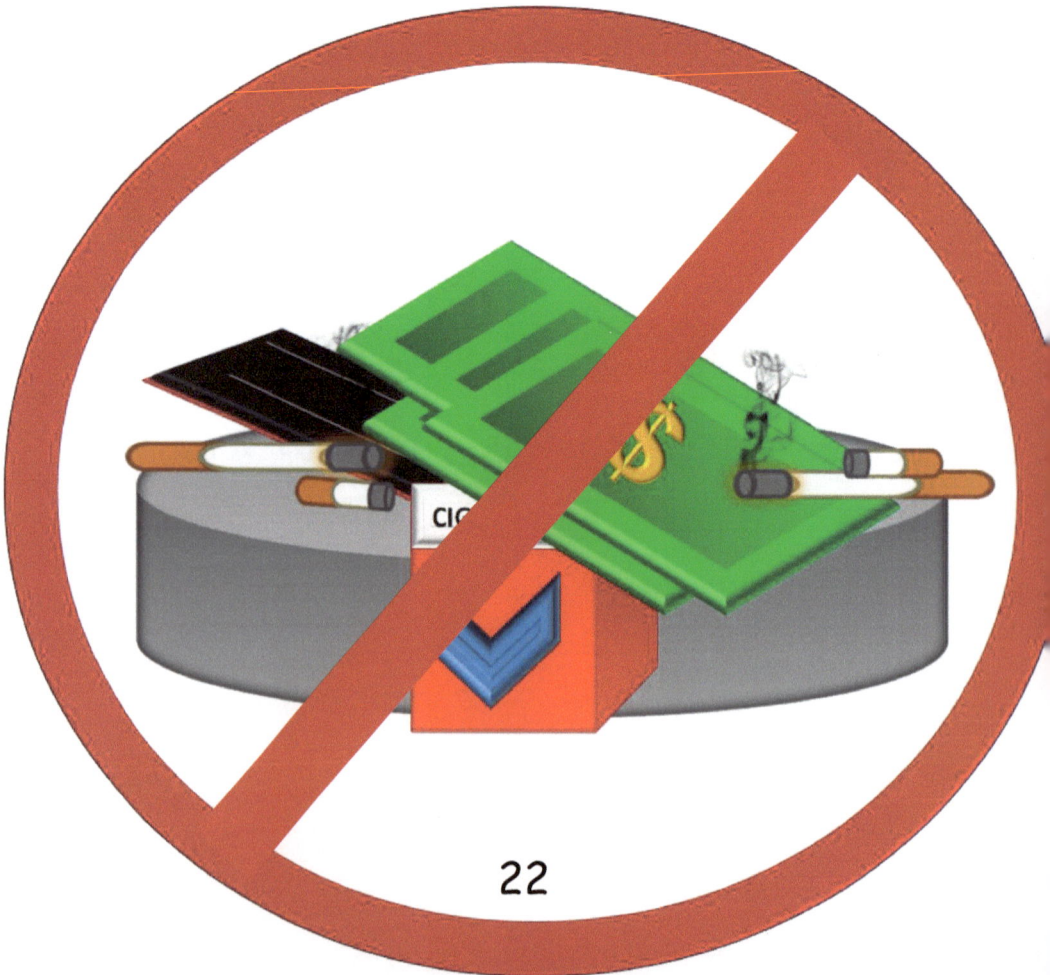

About the Author

Evangelist Jacqueline Charmane is an extremely talented and gifted woman. In 1995, Jacqueline began volunteering nationally and internationally for theatrical productions. It was through freely giving of her time that her talents in theatrical productions and cultural art were cultivated. For nearly twenty years, Jacqueline has written, directed, and performed in stage plays, as well as designed spectacular costumes and dance wardrobes. As Jacqueline worked in theater, her zeal for life and laughter unfolded.

In 1998, Jacqueline began performing gospel comedy that after a decade gave rise to the character "Mother Maeye."Jacqueline (as Mother May-eye") has been seen on *Black Entertainment Television's* (BET) website, over a dozen commercials for the famous gospel talent show *"Sunday Best"*, and has two live DVD recordings. As an author, Jacqueline has written and published eight books and has plans for more. In 2010, Jacqueline branched further out in theater by founding The JC Drama Ministries and has written three plays to date. One thing is for sure, Jacqueline Charmane wisely and uniquely uses her God-given talents.

SPECIAL ACKNOWLEDGEMENTS

Illustration Characters' Contributors:
Oleksii Ovchynnikov @123rf.com
Oleksandr Dvoriankin@123rf.com
oguzaral@123rf.com
Ufuk Uyanik@123rf.com
Artisticco LLC123rf.com
Danilo Sanino@123rf.com
Christos Georghiou@123rf.com
Noratm@123rf.com

chickypooh ™

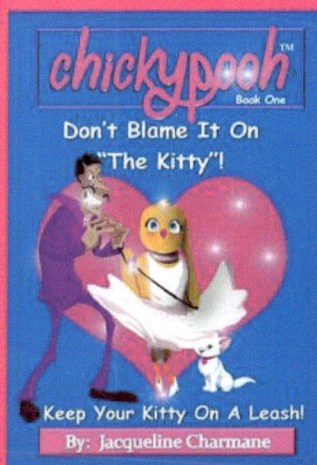

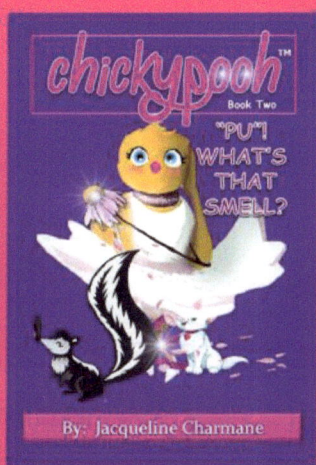

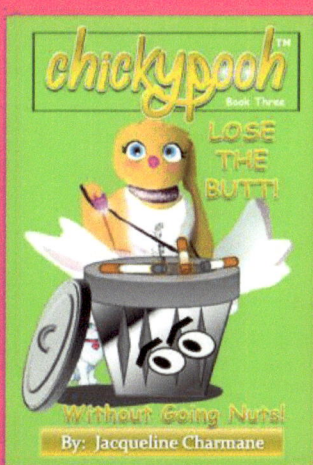

www.ingramcontent.com/pod-product-compliance
Lightning Source LLC
Chambersburg PA
CBHW041805040426

42448CB00001B/44